DEAR,
SINCERELY

PITT POETRY SERIES
Ed Ochester, Editor

DEAR, SINCERELY

DAVID
HERNANDEZ

UNIVERSITY OF
PITTSBURGH
PRESS

Published by the University of Pittsburgh Press, Pittsburgh, Pa., 15260
Manufactured in the United States of America
Printed on acid-free paper
10 9 8 7 6 5 4 3 2 1
ISBN 13: 978-0-8229-6407-0
ISBN 10: 0-8229-6407-4

for Lisa

WE'RE ALL JUST MADE OF
MOLECULES, AND WE'RE
HURLING THROUGH SPACE
RIGHT NOW.

— SARAH
SILVERMAN

CONTENTS

I

II

I

All-American

I'm this tiny, this statuesque, and everywhere
in between, and everywhere in between
bony and overweight, my shadow cannot hold
one shape in Omaha, in Tuscaloosa, in Aberdeen.
My skin is mocha brown, two shades darker
than taupe, your question is racist, nutmeg, beige,
I'm not offended by your question at all.
Penis or vagina? Yes and yes. Gay or straight?
Both boxes. Bi, not bi, who cares, stop
fixating on my sex life, Jesus never leveled
his eye to a bedroom's keyhole. I go to church
in Tempe, in Waco, the one with the exquisite
stained glass, the one with a white spire
like the tip of a Klansman's hood. Churches
creep me out, I never step inside one,
never utter hymns, Sundays I hide my flesh
with camouflage and hunt. I don't hunt
but wish every deer wore a bulletproof vest
and fired back. It's cinnamon, my skin,
it's more sandstone than any color I know.
I voted for Obama, McCain, Nader, I was too
apathetic to vote, too lazy to walk one block,
two blocks to the voting booth. For or against
a woman's right to choose? Yes, for and against.
For waterboarding, for strapping detainees
with snorkels and diving masks. Against burning
fossil fuels, let's punish all those smokestacks
for eating the ozone, bring the wrecking balls,
but build more smokestacks, we need jobs
here in Harrisburg, here in Kalamazoo. Against
gun control, for cotton bullets, for constructing
a better fence along the border, let's raise

concrete toward the sky, why does it need
all that space to begin with? For creating
holes in the fence, adding ladders, they're not
here to steal work from us, no one dreams
of crab walking for hours across a lettuce field
so someone could order the Caesar salad.
No one dreams of sliding a squeegee down
the cloud-mirrored windows of a high-rise,
but some of us do it. Some of us sell flowers.
Some of us cut hair. Some of us carefully
steer a mower around the cemetery grounds.
Some of us paint houses. Some of us monitor
the power grid. Some of us ring you up
while some of us crisscross a parking lot
to gather the shopping carts into one long,
rolling, clamorous and glittering backbone.

Comment Thread in Response to "100 Best Flowers of the Year"

How is hollyhock
better than Delphinium, better than the ruby chandelier
of a Spider lily?

> I agree. Delphiniums rule: blue lace, say a whole
> meadow, thousands
> swaying in Wyoming, say midmorning, lit in that
> champagne light, it doesn't
> get any better.

>> Fuck larkspurs! I'd rather trowel out my eyes
>> and fill both with topsoil
>> than look at those dumb, jumbo
>> pipe cleaners.

Finally Stargazer
cracks the top ten. What a corolla, how plush
and vibrant each petal, Day-Glo flamingo,
a flower so luminous she burns her outline
long after I've closed my lids.
Love, too, how the orange anthers
swivel when nudged
by worker bees.
Praise the lily breeder, Leslie Woodriff,
for bringing Stargazers into the world!
Praise flower shop owners from San Diego to Bangor
who display this hybrid
on their storefront window!

> You have a boner for Stargazers, don't you?

Could someone please tell me where the hell is calla lily?

> Calla lily is doubled-over by a riverbank
> puking milk.

> Calla lily is in the corner of a schoolroom,
> perched atop an idiot's head.

> > No, she's helping a mechanic
> > funnel oil into
> > a Ford Pinto.

First of all, calling
bird of paradise best flower
is a complete misnomer. Second of all, not including
lantana on this list
renders it irrelevant.

> > Your use of misnomer is
> > a misnomer.

If lotus isn't #1 then it's a stupid list. Simple.

> > I agree
> > if by lotus you mean
> > dahlia. There are no blooms
> > more magnificent, not even
> > close. Imperial Wine
> > and Creekside Volcano. Tahiti
> > Sunrise, Wildcat, Solar Flare.

If you need empirical evidence
of God's existence, look
no further than
the mandala of the dahlia.

        God = orchid
        Enough said

                If you need empirical evidence
                of hyperbole's existence,
                see above.

these "best of" lists should be alphabetical
so everyone would stop
bitching about which
flower is better
than which.
reading your opinions is like
face-planting into a pincushion cactus.

        That would place
        Amaryllis
        first, zinnia
        last. How is that
        just?

                you're missing the point
                completely.

What you people don't know about beauty could fill the universe.

Here's the thing with cherry blossoms: collectively
they dazzle, they firework a park.
But one
sprouting from a branch?
Ho-hum. No more glorious than a buttercup.
If buttercups, if daisies
flowered on trees, they would make
this list. If bottle caps, too.

If silk cherry blossoms.

If disposable razors.

If 9V batteries.

If ice cubes.

If light.

In my mother's coffin
we placed a white
chrysanthemum, always
her favorite.

Dear Death

Cool cloak. So goth. I dig how the pleats
ripple like pond water when you move,
and the hood shadows the absence of your face.
Sweet scythe, too. The craftsmanship
of the wooden handle, how smooth the slow
curve. I had to look it up—it's called
the *snath* (rhymes with wrath), or *snathe*
(rhymes with bathe). I prefer the latter, the long
a. Snath sounds like an infectious disease
I might've caught if my mother wasn't there
to steer me from the gutter, from large
puddles marbled green, mosquitoes
scribbling above. How many times
do mosquitoes do your dirty work anyway?
Versus fleas? Versus gunpowder?
How bone-tired were you in Tōhoku?
The previous year in Haiti? Have you ever felt
the sepia wind of remorse? I have 77 more
questions for you, give or take, you're often
in my thoughts. Yesterday, while grinding
coffee beans. While cleaning the lint trap.
Dicing cilantro. Buying ink cartridges.
Clipping my beard. I could go on and on,
you're that legendary in my head.
It works this way: I'm running the knife
across the cutting board, the cilantro
breaks into confetti, I remember my mother
scattering the herb over a Chilean dish, then
her voice on Monday, "numbness in my leg,"
"congestive heart failure," and it fails,

my mind fast-forwards to when it fails,
I can't help it, you grip her IV'd hand, pull her
over, and it is done, her silence begins
blowing through in waves, icing the room—
the thought seized me so completely, the knife
hovered still above the wooden board.
Seriously though, cool cloak. Sick black
fabric. I heard if you turn it inside out,
the whole world's embroidered on the lining.

Figures

The math. He calculated
at his desk, in November's chrome light
slanting through his office window: taxes paid
against the price of one Reaper drone
divided by federal budget.

He found the numbers online,
photos of the aircraft, its fuselage
narrow and windowless, a bone
sheared lengthwise. Then a video:

five in the crosshairs.

Infrared will make anything carrying heat
black. He thought, *five black seeds*
slipping along the dirt trail.
It made watching easier. One walked ahead
or four lagged behind, one

smaller than the rest, which he wished
he hadn't noticed. The explosion
looked like a black bouquet falling away
down the center of his monitor.

Black bouquet too, he thought.

If I tell myself it was just four cents,
I miscalculated, it was three, if I tell myself
my pennies went to another drone,
I chipped in for flight, not flame.
The light beside him brightened

and he gave his eyes to the window, the wind
behind the window, the wind diving
across the street, shaking up the neighbor's oak.
The leaves. He could not stop

witnessing their letting go.

As the History Teacher Lectures on World War I

One student hears "mustard gas" and wonders
if the air smelled like French's or Grey Poupon.
One chews his pencil like a chicken bone.
One executes a stickman in the margins.
Under the blond awning of bangs, one writes
in pink ink a love note to the quarterback.
One is stoned. One sniffs Wite-Out
until his desk ripples. One lifts the trapdoor
of a scab and licks his wound like a postage stamp.
One fidgets in his sleep as if rodents
tread over his flesh. One folds and folds
a sheet of paper until it flies. With spit wads,
one gives pimples to the blackboard.
We must learn from history or be doomed
to repeat it, the teacher says. One hears
the clock biting its fingernails beside the flag.

Dear Professor

Let me explain my lengthy absence—
My entire family got food poisoning,
myself included. We had eaten rotten
fish tacos, old bad cod, I've never been so
nauseous, the house wouldn't stop
spinning, wouldn't stop shuffling
its windows, I was gushing from
I'll spare you the details. And Grandma
shutting down, hallucinating, said the world
was pixilated. We rushed her to St. Mary's
on a flat tire, no spare in the trunk,
a burst of sparks as the screaming rim
scored the road like a pizza cutter.
They plugged her in, her monitor drew
neon green mountain ranges. Strange,
you'd think they'd have Internet access
there, free wi-fi, a wing in the hospital
to check one's email. Odd, too, no
connectivity back home, no electric blood
sluicing through the wires, a hitch
in the system, some inexplicable glitch,
impossible for me to get a hold of you
until now, two weeks after the due date.
I'm sorry. And sorry I missed class today,
another flat tire, stupid overturned
box of nails on the freeway, I hissed
for miles, the car listed, such a headache,
and still queasy from the tacos. Please
consider all this when grading my essay
(see attachment). Please excuse any typos

or logical fallacies, my mind has been
elsewhere: Grandma's mountains
stretched flat. Her green horizon. I want
to live forever. I want to pass your class
and graduate, get a gig, marry some hottie,
see the world, drive until my wheels
come wobbling off, and keep driving—
but first I need to pass your class.
No pressure. Honestly. No pressure.

We Real Nerds

after Gwendolyn Brooks

We real nerds. We
Love words. We

Break lines. We
Trim vines. We

Craft poems. We
Tall gnomes. We

Can't dance. We
Hold stance. We

Reread. We
Wear tweed. We

Small herd. We
Tenured. We

Got smarts. We
Fat hearts. We

Prolong. We
Live long.

Parking FAQ

Q.   Why do I have to pay for parking?
A.   To maintain the lots, fill cracks
     and potholes, we need money for that,
     and money to repaint all
     those parallel lines, all those arrows,
     mow the islands, plant annuals,
     perennials, and keep
     electricity in the evening humming
     down rows and rows of lampposts.
     Otherwise, vehicles
     weaving over a rutted field,
     the chaos of night class.

Q.   Where can I park?
A.   Lots A, C, G, S, 11–20,
     and the area across University Drive,
     behind the tracking houses, strip mall,
     grassland, beyond
     the mountains,
     designated by this sign:

Q.   Is that someone
       flying with a short cape?
       A disembodied moustache?
A.   Look again: a backpacked student
       crawling to class,
       a vulture roving above.

Q.   My friend is leaving campus. Can I
       use his permit?
A.   Only if you wear his clothes
       and attend his classes.
       Only if you foam your mouth
       with his toothbrush
       and dream his dreams.

Q.   This not so much a
       question but a
       complaint about the
       proliferation and
       height of the
       speed bumps and
       how going over
       them they
       rattle my teeth.
A.   Wear a mouthguard.

Q.   Can I wait in the aisles
       for a parking stall to open?
A.   When in your life are you not
       waiting for something?
       You wait for the lecture
       to end, movie to begin, email to arrive,

microwave to beep, neighbor's dog
to quit howling, sex to ripple
across your ravenous flesh. You waiting
for a parking stall is a pint of waiting
in the ocean of waiting
whereupon your heart circles
like an orphaned whale.
In short, ride a bicycle to campus.

Q. I can't walk from the parking lot
     because my leg is in a cast.
     What should I do?
A. First, have the Provost sign your cast.
     Second, have the Vice Provost
     verify the signature.
     Third, from the Dean of Engineering
     check out a dolly cart. Fourth,
     have the Secretary of Health & Human Services
     roll you from class to class.

Q. I don't want to drive to campus.
     What are my alternatives?
A. Walking. The aforementioned bicycle.
     The bus. Razor scooter.
     Thirty years from now a father
     will tell his teenage son,
     Back in the day I got to school
     on a razor scooter.
     His son in turn will picture the longest
     grooves in pavement, wiggling
     over sidewalks and crosswalks,
     the vandalism of moving forward.

Q.   What should I do if my car
won't start?

A.   Sounds like you're in a horror film.
Listen for zombies. Sounds like monks
chanting. Check your side mirror,
rearview mirror, pray the engine catches
before you try the ignition again,
blind spot. They should be
stumbling closer, closer, each one
slightly pigeon-toed.

Q.   Your sarcasm isn't helpful, your answers
aren't answers, your answers suggest
a wound underneath, I'm taking
psychology this semester, love it,
love the unpeeling that goes on,
sometimes a wound is underneath, why
won't you help me?

A.   Because I need help myself.
There are days I'm looking for
something—a book, say—walk
into a room and forget
I was looking for a book, days
I wear a jacket of dread and take
a pill or two. Underneath
there's a wound, on and off since I was six
I've sensed menace in the air,
atoms holding knives,
sometimes no pills
but a tumbler of bourbon, the slow
dissolve of one cube.

Q.   Hey, are you okay?

A.   Better than this morning,
        worse than Tuesday, as forlorn
        as a child who knows
        the kite's not coming back.

Q.   Tell you what, let me make you
        some hot cocoa, nana's recipe,
        in a squat white mug
        bring you hot cocoa.
        The smell alone, oh man
        the smell alone will swaddle your bones.
        Can I bring you a mug?
        The rich scent and uptwisting
        wisps of steam?

A.   I'm moved by your offer,
        the warm gust of your compassion
        despite my unhelpfulness.
        This is not so much an answer
        but rather me wishing each time
        you tap your horn
        a parking stall opens magically,
        me wishing your car battery
        never dies, you have one of those
        vampire batteries, lucky you,
        lucky life
        mile after mile.

Sincerely, the Sky

Yes, I see you down there
looking up into my vastness.

What are you hoping
to find on my vacant face,

there within the margins
of telephone wires?

You should know I am only
bright blue now because of physics:

molecules break and scatter
my light from the sun

more than any other color.
You know my variations—

azure at noon, navy by midnight.
How often I find you

then on your patio, pajamaed
and distressed, head thrown

back so your eyes can pick apart
not the darker version of myself

but the carousel of stars.
To you I am merely background.

You barely hear my voice.
Remember I am most vibrant

when air breaks my light.
Do something with your brokenness.

Dear Proofreader

You're right. I meant "midst," not "mist."
I don't know what I was stinking,
I mean thinking, soap speaks intimately
to my skin every day. Most days.
Depending if darkness has risen
to my skull like smoke up a chimney floe.
Flue. Then no stepping nude
into the shower, no mist turning
the bathroom mirror into frosted glass
where my face would float
coldly in the oval. Picture a caveman
encased in ice. Good. I like how
your mind works, how your eyes
inside your mind works, and your actual eyes
reading this, their icy precision, nothing
slips by them. Even now I can feel you
hovering silently above these lines,
hawkish, Godlike, each period
a lone figure kneeling in the snow.
That's too solemn. I would like to send
search parties and rescue choppers
to every period ever printed.
I would like to apologize to my wife
for not showering on Monday and Tuesday.
I was stinking. I was simultaneously
numb and needled with anxiety,
in the midst of a depressive episode.
Although "mist" would work too,
metaphorically speaking, in the *mist* of,
in the *fog* of, this gray haze that followed me
relentlessly from room to room
until every red bell inside my head
was wrong. Rung.

Poem Beginning with a Line from Robert Hass

All the new thinking is about loss.
This makes me sad. Not the weeping
kind of sad, but the dry-eyed variety,
like when I try recalling the last time
I spoke to my brother or sister. Drifted,
we say, as if it was all the wind's doing,
swelling our sails. Our closeness
was lost. Which is why I'd like to think

there is at least one philosopher
breathing on this January morning
who can dismantle all the large ideas
surrounding our existence, reassemble them
one two three, then look at me
kindly across my little kitchen table,
over the constellation of crumbs,
and say, "Loss does not exist."

Correction: I'd like to think
there is more than one truth-seeker
who has come to this conclusion, a ballroom
full of pointy beards and muttonchops
and handlebar mustaches
or whatever facial hair is fashionable now
within the philosophy community,
it doesn't matter, so long as there's a throng
of these logicians, that they meet
weekly to share their ideas,
none of which is the concept that loss

is all there is. Unless it is the theory of
the loss of loss. What would that look like
stapled onto a telephone pole?

Name: Loss
Breed: Human suffering
Color: Light smothered in ash
Age: Too many millenniums to count

What would a person—say, a woman
wearing earbuds and jogging in the bright sun
who was recently enlightened by
the No Loss principle, the All Gain doctrine,
whatever you want to call it—
what would she think
bouncing by such a flyer? Would her lips
flare into a smile? Would it not
have been there already?
Would the song be less beautiful in her ears
now that heartache was not an issue?

I'm sorry I'm asking so many questions.
I'm thinking we sometimes think too much,
how unseasonably warm it is for January,
that it has been too long since I've said
hello to my parents, longer my siblings.
Wind and road guided them all to Florida
while I stayed in California, both states being
the muttonchops of America
if you are one of those people who sees
faces where there are none.

We Would Never Sleep

We the people, we the one
times 320 million, I'm rounding up, there's really
too many grass blades to count,
wheat plants to tally, just see
the whole field swaying from here to that shy
blue mountain. Swaying
as in rocking, but also the other
definition of the verb: we sway, we influence,
we impress. Unless we're asleep,
the field's asleep, more a postcard
than a real field, portrait of the people
unmoved. You know that shooting last week?
I will admit the number dead
was too low to startle me
if you admit you felt the same,
and the person standing by you
agrees, and the person beside that person.
It has to be double digits,
don't you think? To really
shake up your afternoon? I'm troubled by
how untroubled I felt, my mind's humdrum
regarding the total coffins, five
if you care to know, five still
even if you don't. I'm angry
I'm getting used to it, the daily
gunned down, pop-pop on Wednesday,
Thursday's spent casings
pinging on sidewalk. It all sounds
so industrial, there's nothing metal
that won't make a noise, I'm thinking every gun
should come with a microphone,
each street with loudspeakers
to broadcast their banging.

We would never sleep, the field
always awake, acres of swaying
up to that shy blue mountain, no wonder
why it cowers on the horizon, I mean
look at us, look with the mountain's eyes,
we the people
putting holes in the people.

Master Sommelier Blind-Tastes a Glass of Water

for Shara McCallum

This glass: Did you rinse it?
I ask because there's sediment
swirling like a time-lapse of a galaxy
if stars were debris
without their shining.

So you rinsed it. With gutter water
I presume, then dried it
with a mechanic's rag.
Then it's tap.

Now on to the nose:
the chlorine is
overwhelming, wow, who
shoved me into a swimming pool?
It's positively tap. I'm also picking up
some witchgrass
and moneywort, it's not
easy with all this sodium chloride
assaulting my sinuses. Penny,
I'm detecting old penny, a hint
of natural gas. I have to say
I am
hesitant to taste this.

Here it goes:
O, damn
my astute taste buds! There is definitely
chlorine in this ghastly thing
I refuse to call water. It's just bleach,
weeds, petrol, brass, but
mostly bleach. No mineral notes
whatsoever.

I'm going tap
from a brass faucet, from a region
ruined by fracking. This is
New World, possibly United States
or Brazil. I'm calling
United States, Pennsylvania,
Laurel Highlands, 2013 vintage.

I have to say: This faucet you found?
The small town where you found it?
Their mayor does not
love them enough.

The Prophecies of B. B. Guthrie

I

In the seventh month of the year 2024, thereabouts,
In the Kingdom where the great eagle drags his shadow
Over speed eating competitions, gun shows, and Botox parties,
From the sky will come angels spewing embalming fluid.

II

Venus in Capricorn, Jupiter in Aquarius and Leo,
Mayor Dupree in striped suspenders and wingtip Oxfords:
Each Confederate tree that granted a branch for lynching
Will be whipcracked to splinters by lightning strikes.

III

From the North, a mighty frost and exodus of caribou,
The Four Leaders chiseled on a mount donning snowy wigs.
From the South, a plague of locusts will dim the daylight
And stipple driveway after driveway like pages of prose.

IV

The vainglorious will begin speaking in Goat Latin.
On television screens the anus-bleached starlet will cry out:
Ymoy agentwoy oppedstoy answeringwoy ymoy allscoy!
Sixteen in Applebee's will spontaneously combust.

V

These high-def visions unblurring from a steamed mirror
While the shower drain whispers to me in tongues:
The day will arrive and I will say unto you, *What did I say?*
Believers will construct shelters. Skeptics, bookcases.

VI

On the island of Vineyard belonging to one Martha
A flyby asteroid towing high winds will leave in its wake
Demagnetized credit cards, scattered lobster bibs
And floppy garden hats, a lost terrier named Jenkins.

VII

By one to one ratio, for every Cherokee or Chippewa
Slain by sword or musket, for every Navajo, Apache, Sioux,
Any of the First Residents felled by ancient weaponry,
Their stoic face will materialize on someone else's body.

VIII

In a fortnight the ground will moan like a galleon at sea.
New mountains will surface, old ones muscled aside.
The earth-shaken dead will rise, rise, rise, drop
Behind washcloths begrimed with cemetery soil.

IX

Pestilence will descend upon the land, famine, cannibalism,
Dial-up Internet, nuclear fallout, Rothko horizon:
You will say unto me, *Why o why did I build this*
Skylight on my bunker? What now will fall upon my eyes?

X

The Kingdom, its hour come round at last, goes dark:
Lattice of Christmas lights popping from coast to coast.
God will step into a time machine, reboot the universe.
Boom and all this shrapnel glimmering around us now.

Anyone Who Is Still Trying

Any person, any human, any someone who breaks
      up the fight, who spackles holes or FedExes
ice shelves to the Arctic to keep the polar bears
      afloat, who talks the wind-rippled woman
down from the bridge. Any individual, any citizen
      who skims muck from the coughing ocean,
who pickets across the street from antigay picketers
      with a sign that reads, GOD HATES MAGGOTS,
or, GOD HATES RESTAURANTS WITH ZAGAT RATINGS
      LESS THAN 27. Any civilian who kisses
a forehead heated by fever or despair, who reads
      the X ray, pins the severed bone. Any biped
who volunteers at soup kitchens, who chokes
      a Washington lobbyist with his own silk necktie—
I take that back, who gives him mouth-to-mouth
      until his startled heart resumes its kabooms.
Sorry, I get cynical sometimes, there is so much
      broken in the system, the districts, the crooked
thinking, I'm working on whittling away at this
      pessimism, harvesting light where I can find it.
Any countryman or countrywoman who is still
      trying, who still pushes against entropy,
who stanches or donates blood, who douses fires
      real or metaphorical, who rakes the earth
where tires once zeroed the ground, plants something
      green, say spinach or kale, say a modest forest
for restless breezes to play with. Any anyone
      from anywhere who considers and repairs,
who builds a prosthetic beak for an eagle—
      I saw the video, the majestic bird disfigured

by a bullet, the visionary with a 3-D printer,
     with polymer and fidelity, with hours
and hours and hours, I keep thinking about it,
     thinking we need more of that commitment,
those thoughtful gestures, the flight afterward.

The New

If forty is the new thirty then ten is
the new infant. Housing development
a coyote roaming a hillside
swaying with windblown foxtail.
New wave is the new grunge, disco
the new new wave,
but punk is still punk.

You reading this
is no longer you reading this
but rather your eyes a decade ago
skating down a menu:
Burger
Tuna Melt
Turkey Club
BLT
Who eats tuna melt these days?
What is the lifespan
of albacore, the ones that dart
past the net? I miss my dead grandparents

who are the new grandparents
alive and coughing
in a nursing home, its doilies
the wool of unborn sheep.
In the waiting room, my long
eyelashed nephew
napped across blue sofa chairs,
dream-twitching.

Rain is the new ocean.
The ocean, the new rain.

Building a Joke

In the season before trees begin
their ritual of swapping green for rust,
a DC-9 airliner and Cessna
collided over the city where I grew up.
This isn't funny, but comedians will tell you
laughter is possible with any tragedy
if one waits long enough, time
and timing are key. It's been 27 years
since I stood alone in the backyard
beside our family's orange tree,
stood within its scent and looked
northeast to witness the smoke
blocks away and not the televised one,
delayed seven seconds.

Clarity, too, is necessary, I cannot say
somebody noticed something
near the crash site. I will tell you instead
Anita saw a hand lying on Carmenita Road
and believed it was fake, given
how pristine the severing,
given the manicured fingernails,
unchipped, painted the palest crimson.
Weeks later, while passing a joint
at Regional Park, she said she thought
it was a mannequin's. With enough distance
it might've seemed we were taking turns
stitching the night, there on the topmost
row of the bleachers.

Time and clarity, also a setup that tightens
the coiled spring of a punch line: so, there is
this handless mannequin

wandering around the wreckage, sifting,
when one of the firemen on location says,
I mean one of the policemen says,
one of the medics, the coroners I mean,
when one of the reporters holding
a microphone like a charred ice cream cone,
when one Henri Bergson, the French philosopher,
says, "Comedy can only begin at the point
where our neighbor's personality
ceases to affect us. It begins, in fact,
with what might be called a growing
callousness to social life."

This still isn't funny, I know. I'm missing
the basic tools to build this joke
or not but cannot drill
so many holes through my conscience.
I should've made something else
entirely, a white heron
folded from paper or paper from a fallen tree
or crutches to prevent it from falling
in the first place, that's what
my mother did, homemade crutches
out of dowel rods
so the orange tree's branches wouldn't bow, touch
grass, they were that
abundant with fruit, around July, August,
she would deliver some
to Gordon and Joan across the street.

Thirteen

Midsummer, always a moaning at home
the week before my grandfather's knee surgery,
always the listless crawling of June bugs
along the windowsills.
Summer of mumbling *dios mío*, summer of no
stairs, no ascending at all, so we pushed aside
the dining room table, maneuvered in
the king bed. He dreamed below
a cheap chandelier like an anchor
just risen from water, the clear drops caught
mid-falling.
Late evening, blue shadows—
I watched TV alone, the volume low. The walls
glowed in Technicolor, sunk to black
between commercials. This is me
stalling, this is me resisting
confession, a June bug thumping
against the window. Another. This is me
couch-sprawled, this is
the sound of my grandfather
groaning, the chiseled anguish on his face
surfacing from the darkness
of the foyer. This is him limping
to the bathroom with fire
in his knee, glass in his knee, a labored
breathing. Do you see him? Do you see
the boy, frozen in the ancient light
of suffering?
                    I want to go back,
yank him to his feet. I want to tell him
about shame, that heavy
red bird, how long it lives in the mind,

the heart, years, decades, the weight
of it when it settles down, turning
your whole body into its perch.
That boy, I would make him listen.
And he would go to him—his mother's father,
his blood and root—and offer
a lifted arm, curved
like the end of a banister rail.

How frightened I was then, and how foolish
I am now, thinking this admission
would reconcile myself
with my younger self.
That boy. This long silence
between us. This guilt he brought to me.
This red feather in my hand.

Sincerely, Blue Blood

It is a myth. Never mind
    how it looks by observing
        the underside of your wrist.
    Your blood, deoxygenated,
        is not my shade.

To find my kind of vital fluid,
    go to the ocean and into
        the bodies of certain creatures.
    Go to oysters, to octopi.
        Take a crab, hack it

open, and you will see me
    marbling the cutting board.
        Forget how it appears
here on the tender meat below
        your thumb: I do not travel

your veins. There is no indigo
    going to and from your heart.
        Even at your bluest, when you
look too long at your wrist.
        I have nothing to do with it.

Dear Mockingbird

Damn the intelligence of your eyesight
for puzzling out Diego's stripes
in the crisscross of branch shadows.
Damn your birdcall, your bursts
of static, some mechanical thing
breaking down. Your wings, too—
damn them both, fanning open audaciously
when you plummet, dragging your screech
right over him, then fly skyward
only to dive again, all without pausing
your song. Did I say song? I mean needle
scraping across a vinyl record.
I mean shut the fuck up, skedaddle,
let my cat be, who swipes the air
where you passed, again and again
where you passed, always half a second
too late. It's sad watching him
fail repeatedly, and comical,
also mundane, which eventually becomes
sublime, there's this sensation
like my mind is traveling
around a Möbius strip, which means
I've been watching too long.
Can I make a confession?
I stack words on top of words to push away
loneliness, though it comes back
and I build another mound.
You see my dilemma. No you don't.
I understand you don't understand
anything I've said, there's no
mockingbird translator here
to facilitate a useful discussion.

I am, more or less, talking to myself.
It's something we humans do
when the universe feels
as large and cold as it is.

Sincerely, Paper Gown

Of course I am blue, falling
somewhere on the spectrum
            between powder and slate.

I know what you are
            thinking: *Why not green,*
why not orange, why not

            Velcro instead of
these impossible to tie
            tie-backs, why fatigue

and shortness of breath and this
            feeling there's a gyroscope
whirling in my head?

            You sigh and fidget.
Your palms whisper
            down my papered length

over your thighs. No mirror
            to see how you look.
Slouched, the stalks of your legs

            dangling over the exam table.
Wilted comes to mind.
            A lone morning glory

bending underneath the current
            from a weed whacker.
Look at me. From knees to throat

I am here to calm you.
What better hue is there to smooth
the breakers in your blood?

Ode to Morphine

I.

I'm confined
in my own sunny living room—rigid, supine,

a toppled mannequin in plaid pajama bottoms
beside the ottoman,

the sky through
double-paned sliding glass that electric blue

which, looking at it, forces you to squint.
Any movement—

my back flares
above the pelvis like some diabolical flower

unfurling steely petals. One cloud floats by.
One more. The sky

looks too good,
too postcardish, the sun lavishing the boxwood

clipped into a green column, gleefully upright.
I'm skintight

in my own body,
this wretched sack of cells, nothing but a cruddy

version of myself. I see Lisa's worried face,
eyes uppercase.

We're going
to urgent care, she says. I turn sideways, lowing

like a speared bull. I want to be a cloud in the sun.
That one. That one.

2.

O sweet syringe of modern medicine   O benevolent doctor

who thumbed the plunger   what blooming around my bones

what light   O glowing blood flowing   through my floating limbs

at last I'm a cloud   lying on the sectional couch

I think I'm a cirrostratus   or cirrus   my head feels

that wispy   that windblown when I lift it   when Lisa says   *O my god*

look at that raccoon   I lift it   open languid lids

and through the rippled air   beyond the sliding glass

I spot him   in the plum-colored dusk   lumbering atop

our wooden fence   across the length of it   a blindfolded   four-legged

high-wire walker   the ringed and downy tail   bobbing behind

O this world   O to be alive in it   with any given body

Mayfly

I died. I was
born the day before,
floated up inside

a globe of air
to the water's
wobbling roof.

I molted, opened
ghostly wings,
was soon

airborne
with my brothers,
one dot

on the stippled cloud.
We mobbed
above the river,

we eddied,
desire rousing
in each of us.

Every time
a mate arrived,
she left latched

onto another.
So went the minutes,
the river scrolling

endlessly. By dusk,
while the sky's
lush blue

drained out
quicker,
I felt my life

ending. It could
not have been
any fuller.

Sincerely, the Blue Jay

When you were a boy.
When you had a box

propped up on a stick, a long,
long string tethered to it.
On the grass twenty yards
out, in the shadow

below the box, some bread
your little fingers

broke. One hour into the next
you waited, testing
the string. Inside your home,
lightning before a door

thundered closed. Then I
spoke, scissoring down

from June's tulip blue.
I am telling you this
as if you have forgotten
how I dashed past the box,

unfooled, and stood
coolly in the shade

beneath the orange tree.
Recall the breeze. Recall
the window and its reflection,
puzzle of clouds

over your mother's face,
the string shivering before

wind kicked over your box.
Below the plump globes of fruit,
I startled, opened
cobalt wings, flew.

Dear Doorknob

I turned you and you slipped off—cold, heavy

      brass in my bewildered hand
      as your counterpart

dropped on the other side, baritone clunk
against the hardwood,
         nothing to say but
      what rose to my lips: "Whoops."

I wobbled from wine, so

         sliding your spindle
back
through the spindle hub

wasn't easy, the other guests
tipsy in the living room, oblivious

      to my clumsy handiwork—*that goes into*
this that
        way—No,
   like this.

      There is a click, a round
      gold sound that tells me

I fixed you.

O, if only
you could return the favor, repair this
            small defect of my mind,

some shoddy
        wiring with the on/off switch
        that sinks me

        mercilessly into darkness
            no matter where the sun is.

Yesterday a Mylar Balloon

coasted down my street,
its heart-shaped head
bulbous and mirroring
the houses, the trees. It
swiveled as it sailed.

The stretched red ribbon
was as tall as me, its medallion
weight scraped the pavement.
Into a busier street the wind
pushed it, then the wind

of two-lane traffic
yanked the balloon this way,
the other. It wove
in between the vehicles,
its gilded skin flaring in the sun.

It hopped and zigzagged
all the way to the sidewalk
and stopped, bobbing
in jacaranda shade.
In no time did anyone

come to claim it. I
waited, forehead resting
against my office window.
So long in that position
I stirred up longing.

Self-Portrait as Team Mascot

I do not speak—

my head lodged inside the cougar's throat.
Midway up the neck, meshed eyeholes.
So I only see what's right in front: the bleachers
but not the scoreboard. The goalpost
but not the bleachers. There is no

whole picture anymore.
By summer, by halftime,
I'm burning inside this thing, my entire body
glossed with sweat, and I am
more like a garden slug
than the animal I'm zippered inside.

But I am human, see. I'm just
as worried and lonely as you.

Look, the brunette over there,
the one holding the cheerleader cone—
when I say her name
to myself, my mind slides
down this tube, it goes

and goes and soon my heart
follows, and I swear I can almost
smell the green apples
in whatever glorious shampoo
she lathers into her hair.

A whistle shrills. The players huddle.
Before the howling crowd
I strut, lift a paw beside my tilted head,
as in: *I cannot hear you.*
When I turn around, she's in my eyesight

way on the other end. Like a struck match
her stadium-lit hair
wavers in the night wind.

Inside this thing, I am burning.

Sincerely, the Cat's Eye

First the feline
comes to you, cloud white,
one-eyed, then I
look at you: blue iris, cool
icy ring of me,
the pupil's dark seed.

Cat first, me next, then this
thought in your head:
How did the vet remove it?
Some little spoonlike tool,
then the other eye looking
up from a surgical tray, the cornea
torn in a catfight.

So one thought
follows another follows a third
until you equate
my twin to the damaged world.
Bomb craters. Wildfires. Giant
wedges of white
toppling into the Arctic. Trees,
acres of trees, felled
by chainsaw, by tsunami.
The earth grinding into itself,
leveling what was once

upright. Stop it. When you are
like this, obsessed
with disaster, I would rather be
ten time zones away from you—

a child's marble in Moscow.
But I am stuck here
until this cat uncoils from your lap.
Let us make the best of this
moment together.
See how I dazzle like sapphire
under a jeweler's lamp?
Just look at me.

No, the other one.

Black Site

You and I, we only have a few more weeks to speak. Yesterday was all a runaround. One story told a dozen ways. One story drawing and erasing its own face.

> *My arms. I cannot*
> *feel them anymore, anchored up*
> *the way you have them,*
> *however many weeks*
> *standing like this. You have taken my arms,*
> *insulated the sleeves*
> *somehow with clouds.*
> *My legs, too. I am*
> *floating, ballooned. Is this*
> *healthy to you?*

I'm not a physician, but you appear healthy to me. In the pink, as we Americans like to say. I can tell by your coloring, by the spring in your voice, that you have received the best medical care.

> *No, I have not. You have*
> *not been here to witness*
> *what the doctors*
> *do not do.*
> *How little they scribble*
> *on their clipboards.*
> *How they leave me*
> *alone with the icy flowers*
> *of their cologne.*
> *You have stolen my arms, legs,*
> *rolled my eyes*
> *into the blackest tunnel.*

No, we haven't. You have everything. Arms, legs. They are still with you.

And my eyes?

Under the hood, yes.

And my tongue?

We've been through this, I've heard this story before. You are here: all of you.

Being here is being
nowhere. I am air.
I am abstract.
Strange how I hear
my voice when I have
no vocal chords or ears, no mind
to weave the wavelengths.
Is this even my voice?

We have been through this.

You have been through nothing.
You have free will.
You have sunlight, grapes, dignity, piano, ice.

And this.

I have suffering upon suffering.

Have you thought about what we discussed yesterday? Before the air-conditioner was turned off, what we discussed?

> *Thought about, yes. Thinking is*
> *all I have here, this bottomless*
> *moment and thinking, a recollection of home*
> *but not its actual walls*
> *sliding underneath my hands,*
> *not my tangible bed*
> *or green teakettle. Only*
> *the memory of them, the thought*
> *of yard, of outside and—*

Grass blades whispering below your feet. I've heard this before. My ears have walked up and down this well-worn path. Your teakettle is no stranger to me.

> *It only whistles in gold.*

About our discussion yesterday. Before we stopped the tape recorder, the air-conditioner. Before doctors were summoned. Before you were fed. Tell me about your affiliation with [REDACTED].

> *It does not matter*
> *how many times or ways*
> *I tell you: he is*
> *unknown to me.*
> *I cannot conjure a face*
> *to latch onto that name*
> *to pin onto a memory.*
> *Above his necktie I see*
> *nothing but nothing.*

We have your conversation with [REDACTED] on tape. We know you know this.

> *I know this: that voice*
> *belongs to someone else.*

If you wish, we can play the tape again.

> *The tape hisses for a reason.*

To jog your memory, if you wish.

> *You will only hear*
> *what is not there. You will call the voice*
> *mine when it lives*
> *in another man's mouth.*
> *You will call a mountain*
> *pebble and tell me to simply*
> *toss it into the sea.*

What is your affiliation?

> *There is nothing to tell, no wings*
> *to lift your sparrows.*

Then the A/C stays off. Then the hood stays on. Then tomorrow runs its knife along the night sky. Then the sun unburies its head. Then we will do this again.

> *Without the hood?*

Depending on what you give us.

> *Every summer my mother*
> *tended her fig tree,*
> *slipped a white bag*
> *over every fruit, cinched*
> *tight around the stem.*

You have told this story before.

> *Otherwise, fruit flies.*
> *By dusk, the sacks*
> *glowed outside*
> *my bedroom window.*
> *White lanterns, dark bulbs.*
> *Their vacant—*

Promise of light.

The Universe

What she says is true or what he says is true
or the answer falls somewhere
in the middle, their discussion wedged
within the crush of bodies on the Q.
The concept of Self is all
an illusion, she says. The mind's
one-way mirror between you
and our communal experience.
The train races over the river, the river
mosaics the sunlight. What are you
saying? he says. That "we" is the only
pronoun allowed in our mouths?
"I" is like an ice pick, each time
you utter it, you break yourself
away from the universe. Here's the flaw
in your reasoning, he says. If I say
I see your point, I'm still saying I.
That's the flaw of language, the boundary
of words. Look, she says, imagine looking
at everyone objectively,
gliding over this train. What am I,
a bird? Yes, a fast pretty starling. Go on.
You would only see the collective we
heading to the city and not single out
yourself. The train jostles. His eyes
slide from face to face, eyes to eyes,
some looking at his looking, some
averting, then his own vaporous face
in the window, laid over
the Lower East Side like acetate.

He turns to her: his squirrely girlfriend.
I'm an I, he says, and you're an I,
and that woman in the red pea coat reading
Isabel Alende is an I, and this kid
on your right, earbudded to rhythm, slow-
nodding yes continuously. I, I, I, she says.
Stop dividing us from the universe.
All right, everyone is part of
the cosmos, kumbaya from here
to Sri Lanka, I'll give you that much.
Don't say part of, you are still
making divisions when you say
part of. How would you say it? She rests
her fingertip at the center of his chest.
This is the universe. She points
to herself. This is the universe. And this kid
flooding his head with music, he says.
Go on. Everyone on the Q. Every
thing, actually: moon dust and navel oranges,
warheads, cardamom seeds, lava piling
over lava. She holds his hand
or he holds hers. Strange, he says,
acknowledging the universe like this, this
moment like this. The universe is strange,
yes, she says. It is beautiful. Too bad it is
destructive, too. It's a pretty bird in flames
flying regardless. The city scrolls
by and by the train windows. Is the universe
takeout at my place tonight? Yes, noodles
swirled in a small white box tonight.

ACKNOWLEDGMENTS

Grateful acknowledgment is made to the following publications in which some of these poems, sometimes in earlier versions, originally appeared:

Blackbird: "Parking FAQ," "The Prophecies of B. B. Guthrie," "Thirteen," "The Universe"; *Boston Review*: "Building a Joke"; *Cave Wall*: "Sincerely, Paper Gown," "Sincerely, the Sky"; *Cincinnati Review*: "As the History Teacher Lectures on World War I," "We Real Nerds"; *The Collagist*: "Self-Portrait as Team Mascot"; *Field*: "Dear Death," "Dear Mockingbird," "Figures," "Mayfly"; *Kenyon Review Online*: "Comment Thread in Response to '100 Best Flowers of the Year'"; *New England Review*: "Master Sommelier Blind-Tastes a Glass of Water," "Sincerely, Blue Blood"; *Poetry Daily*: "All-American," "Dear Doorknob"; *Rattle*: "Dear Proofreader"; *The Rumpus*: "The New"; *Southern Review*: "All-American," "Anyone Who Is Still Trying," "Sincerely, the Blue Jay"; *The Sun*: "We Would Never Sleep"; *Threepenny Review*: "Dear Doorknob"; *Verse Daily*: "Sincerely, the Sky," "We Real Nerds"; *West Branch*: "Sincerely, the Cat's Eye" (as "Blue Rooms"); *Zyzzyva*: "Dear Professor," "Poem Beginning with a Line from Robert Hass."

"All-American" was reprinted in *The Best American Poetry 2013* and *The Pushcart Prize XXXVIII*.

"Dear Professor" was reprinted in *Wide Awake: Poets of Los Angeles and Beyond*.

I would also like to express my gratitude to the National Endowment for the Arts for their generous support during the time some of these poems were written.